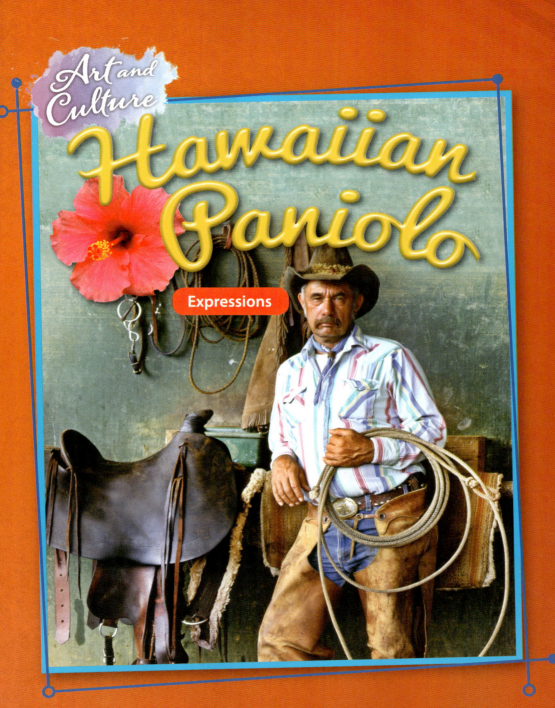

Art and Culture

Hawaiian Paniolo

Expressions

Nicole Sipe

Consultants

Lisa Ellick, M.A.
Math Specialist
Norfolk Public Schools

Pamela Estrada, M.S.Ed.
Teacher
Westminster School District

Publishing Credits

Rachelle Cracchiolo, M.S.Ed., *Publisher*
Conni Medina, M.A.Ed., *Managing Editor*
Dona Herweck Rice, *Series Developer*
Emily R. Smith, M.A.Ed., *Series Developer*
Diana Kenney, M.A.Ed., NBCT, *Content Director*
Stacy Monsman, M.A., *Editor*
Kristy Stark, M.A.Ed., *Editor*
Kevin Panter, *Graphic Designer*

Image Credits: cover, p.1 Kerrick James/Alamy; p.6 (bottom right), p.10 (bottom left), p.11 Granger; p.10 (bottom right) D and S Photographic Services/Alamy; p.12 North Wind Picture Archives/Alamy; p.13, pp.16–17 Mark and Carolyn Blackburn Collection of Polynesian Art/Bridgeman Images; p.14 (both), p.15 courtesy of Paniolo Preservation Society Collection at the North Hawaii Education and Research Center; p.19 (top), p.25 (top left) courtesy of Stella Akana collection of the North Hawaii Education and Research Center collection; p.20 Mark Boster/Los Angeles Times via Getty Images; p.21 Design Pics Inc./Alamy; p.22 (top) J. Anthony Martinez Photography; p.22 (bottom) Photo Resource Hawaii/Alamy; p.24, p.26 (top) Douglas Peebles Photography/Alamy; 25 (top right) Photo Resource Hawaii/Alamy; p.27 (left), p.29 (right) Debra Behr/Alamy; p.27 (right) Bruce C. Murray/Shutterstock; all other images from iStock and/or Shutterstock.

Library of Congress Cataloging-in-Publication Data

Names: Sipe, Nicole, author.
Title: Art and culture : Hawaiian paniolo / Nicole Sipe.
Other titles: Hawaiian paniolo
Description: Huntington Beach, CA : Teacher Created Materials, [2018] | Includes index. | Audience: Grades 4-6.
Identifiers: LCCN 2017033185 (print) | LCCN 2017035284 (ebook) | ISBN 9781425859541 (eBook) | ISBN 9781425858087 (pbk.).
Subjects: LCSH: Hawaii--Social life and customs--Juvenile literature. | Cowboys--Hawaii--Juvenile literature. | Ranch life--Hawaii--Juvenile literature.
Classification: LCC DU624.5 (ebook) | LCC DU624.5 .S53 2018 (print) | DDC 636.2/1309969--dc23
LC record available at https://lccn.loc.gov/2017033185

Teacher Created Materials

5301 Oceanus Drive
Huntington Beach, CA 92649-1030
http://www.tcmpub.com

ISBN 978-1-4258-5808-7
© 2018 Teacher Created Materials, Inc.
Made in China
Nordica.112017.CA21701237

Table of Contents

Aloha, Paniolo 4

The Gift of Cattle 6

Go West, Young Men 12

Head 'Em Up, Move 'Em Out 15

Paniolo Culture.. 20

Paniolo Today.. 24

Problem Solving 28

Glossary 30

Index.. 31

Answer Key... 32

Note to the reader: The Hawaiian language includes a letter that looks like this: '. It is called an 'okina. It signifies a stop between two sounds. Another Hawaiian mark is the kahakō and signifies a long vowel sound.

Aloha, Paniolo

When you think about the Hawaiian Islands, you might think of beautiful beaches. You might picture pineapples growing in a field or volcanoes stretching toward the sky. Perhaps you think of surfers riding waves or hula dancers moving in rhythm. You probably don't picture cowboys, but you should. Cowboys are an important part of Hawai'i. They are as much a part of Hawai'i's culture and history as all the other things you imagined.

Hawaiian cowboys are called paniolo (PAN-ee-oh-loh). Paniolo are a lot like the cowboys you have seen in Western movies or on ranches. They lasso calves. They herd **cattle**. They ride horses. They work on ranches. However, paniolo have a Hawaiian style all their own.

In Hawai'i, you might see paniolo on ranches with flower **leis** (LAYZ) on their hats. You might see paniolo riding horses with Spanish saddles. They may even be wearing **chaps** over their jeans. Paniolo are unique cowboys. Their history makes up a special part of Hawaiian culture.

A hula dancer performs on the beach.

A paniolo rides on horseback at the Aloha Festival's Floral Parade in Honolulu.

The Gift of Cattle

Which came first to Hawai'i: the cowboys or the cattle? (Hint: The right answer has four legs.)

Cattle are not **indigenous** to Hawai'i. They were not always there. All other mammals came by other means. In fact, there are only two **mammals** that are native to the islands: monk seals and hoary bats. Captain George Vancouver was the man who brought cattle to the islands.

Vancouver was an English ship navigator. He sailed all over the western coast of North America. He made several trips to the Hawaiian islands from 1791 to 1794. He sailed over 2,000 miles (3,219 kilometers) across the Pacific Ocean each time. During one trip, Vancouver landed on the beaches of the south side of the Big Island.

Captain George Vancouver

King Kamehameha I

Vancouver brought gifts with him for Hawai'i's king. King Kamehameha (KAH-may-hah-may-hah) I. Curious Hawaiians were waiting when his ship reached land. Vancouver gave the king four cattle, two ewes, and one ram.

These animals were a sight to the Hawaiians! They were the largest land mammals they had ever seen. Some people were excited. But, most people were not happy when the cattle began to eat their crops.

LET'S EXPLORE MATH

Monk seals are native to Hawai'i. During the first few months of their lives, they gain a lot of weight. Use the expressions to compare the total weight (in pounds) of two monk seals at birth and at 2 months old.

- Total weight at birth: $25 + 27$
- Total weight at 2 months old: $8 \times (25 + 27)$

The first cattle did not do well on the island. Some died from illness. Others were killed and eaten by the islanders. So, Vancouver brought King Kamehameha I even more cattle in 1794. After delivering the animals, Vancouver shared an idea with the king. Vancouver suggested that the king place a kapu (KAH-poo) on the animals. This code of conduct was respected by Hawaiians. It would make killing cattle **taboo**. The cattle population would have a chance to grow. They would have even more cattle in the future.

King Kamehameha I agreed. He wanted to make sure that the cattle would be safe on the island. He did not want anyone to kill them. He had the animals moved to a place where they would be alone to live and **reproduce**. It was an **ideal** location near the town of Kona (KOH-nuh) on the Big Island. It was 0.5 mi. (0.8 km) wide, so there was plenty of space. It had lots of grass and watering holes for them to use. The king had people build a stone wall around the area to keep the cattle contained.

The number of cattle increased, just as Hawaiians hoped. However, the cattle learned to escape. Over time, they spread across the Big Island. Cattle continued to multiply. Soon, they were everywhere!

In the summer of 1803, Richard Cleveland brought the first horses to Hawai'i. Cleveland was an American trader. He sailed to Hawai'i on a ship named *Lelia Byrd*. He gave King Kamehameha I two horses, a mare and a foal, from California. Cleveland did not know it at the time, but horses would become very important in the near future.

Meanwhile, about 25,000 wild cattle roamed the Big Island. They were out of control. They wrecked crops. They ate building material on houses. Some even attacked and injured Hawaiians. The problem was going from bad to worse. People were fed up. Something needed to be done!

In 1830, Kamehameha's son, King Kamehameha III, lifted the kapu on killing cattle. People could now hunt or **domesticate** the animals. This helped ease the problem.

Then, the king had another idea. He wanted Hawaiians to start selling beef and **tallow**, or cow fat. He wanted to sell these things to ships that passed through Hawai'i. The king also wanted to create a **ranching** industry in the islands. Hawaiians had never tried ranching before. They were not sure where to start. The king searched for the right people to help with the job.

tallow

Richard Cleveland

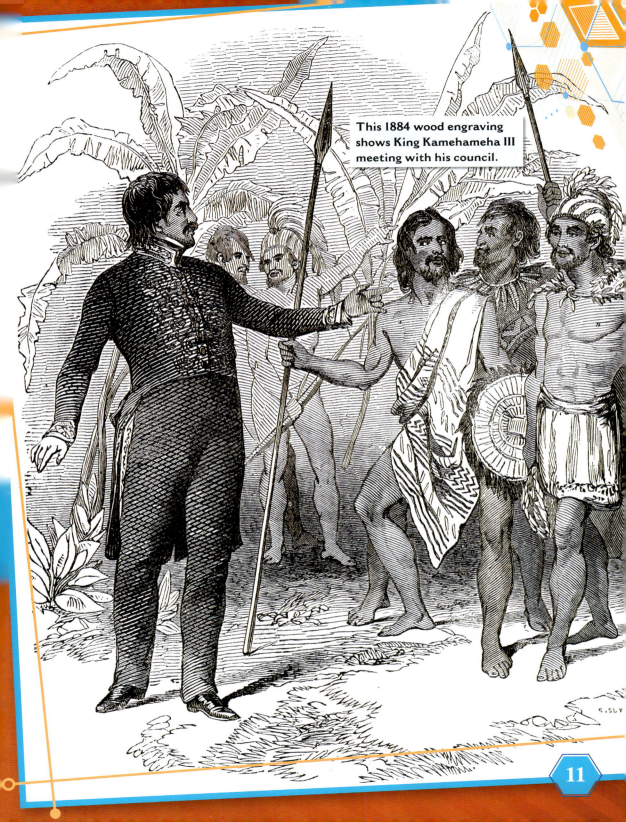
This 1884 wood engraving shows King Kamehameha III meeting with his council.

Go West, Young Men

The king needed cowboys to help with the cattle. He sent his high chiefs to the **mainland** to find some. They were to bring them back to Hawai'i.

His chiefs found three Mexican-Spanish cowboys, called vaqueros (vah-CARE-ohs), from California who could help. These cowboys were named Kossuth, Louzeida, and Ramon. They brought with them the things they needed to do the job. They brought spurs, Spanish-style saddles, and **sombreros**. Most importantly, they brought their own horses. Unlike the wild horses of Hawai'i, these horses knew how to act around cattle. They were familiar with working on a ranch. When Kossuth, Louzeida, and Ramon arrived on the Big Island, they were ready to share their skills with the island people.

a vaquero in the 1800s

Paniolo herd cattle at Parker Ranch in the 1890s.

Hawaiians needed a name for these newcomers. The cowboys spoke Spanish, so Hawaiians called them paniolo. *Paniolo* is the Hawaiian word for *español*, which means "Spanish." The Hawaiian language has 13 letters and does not include the letter *s*. So, they pronounced *español* as *paniolo*. The meaning of *paniolo* has changed over the years. Now, it is a word that describes all cowboys who work in Hawai'i, no matter what language they speak.

LET'S EXPLORE MATH

Alphabets have different numbers of letters. The Hawaiian alphabet has 13 letters, the English alphabet has 26 letters, and the Spanish alphabet has 27 letters. Show how the number of letters in the languages can be related by writing grouping symbols in the equations to make them true.

1. $13 \times 4 - 2 = 26$
2. $26 + 13 \div 3 = 13$
3. $13 - 4 \times 3 = 27$
4. $27 \div 9 - 6 + 4 = 13$

Paniolo herd cattle into pens.

Paniolo use their rope skills to brand cattle.

Head 'Em Up, Move 'Em Out

The original paniolo were in charge of a lot of key tasks. Their first task was to teach Hawaiians how to break, or tame, wild horses. Then, the horses could be used to round up wild cattle on the island. Ranch horses must be able to carry heavy loads, climb over hills, and swim through water. Breaking the horses was essential for getting them ready to work.

Once horses were trained, paniolo had to teach Hawaiians all they knew about ranch work. Hawaiians needed to learn to handle cattle and horses. Learning these skills would help them be successful in the ranching industry. Islanders were eager to learn these new skills.

Rope skills were essential for catching cattle. Paniolo taught Hawaiians how to cut and braid **lariats** (LEHR-ee-uhts), or lassos. Paniolo showed them how to make lariats bigger to catch large steer. Then, they showed Hawaiians how to make them smaller to catch small calves. Lariats made herding cattle easier.

Paniolo pose for a photo at Parker Ranch.

Paniolo lead cattle into the ocean to board a waiting ship in the 1930s.

Paniolo were also very skilled in the water. One of their jobs was to herd cattle onto ships. Ships took cattle to be sold at markets on nearby islands. Cattle were often shipped from the Big Island to O'ahu (oh-AH-hoo), a distance of about 200 mi. (322 km).

Many steps had to be taken to herd cattle from shore to ship. Since salt water can stain, dry, and damage leather, paniolo removed their saddles and boots. They replaced leather saddles with wooden ones. Wooden saddles held up better in the water. Paniolo entered the water barefoot, atop horses with wooden saddles.

Paniolo lassoed cattle one by one. From their horses, paniolo pulled cattle to rowboats that were waiting just off the beach. Horses had to be extremely strong to do this kind of work. They needed **stamina** to work all day in the water.

Sailors in rowboats tied cattle to the sides of the boats. They made sure that the animals were above water so they would not drown. Slowly, they rowed to the awaiting freight ships.

Let's Explore Math

Paniolo had to ship cattle about 200 miles. Which expressions represent 200?

A. $2 \times 5 \times (7 + 4 + 9)$

B. $2 \times 5 \times 7 + 4 + 9$

C. $45 + 55 \times 2$

D. $(45 + 55) \times 2$

E. $10 \times 5 \times 2 + 38 + 62$

F. $10 \times 5 \times (2 + 38) + 62$

Paniolo load cattle onto ships in the 1930s.

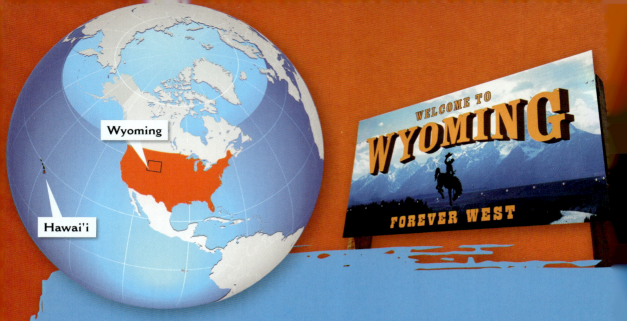

Famous Paniolo

In time, some paniolo became so good at what they did that they became legends in Hawai'i. Three of the most famous paniolo were Ikua (ee-KOO-ah) Purdy, Archie Ka'a'ua (kah-OW-uh), and Jack Low. These three men sailed from Hawai'i to the mainland in 1908. Their destination was a rodeo in Wyoming. It was the biggest rodeo in the United States. Only the best cowboys competed at this yearly event.

The paniolo entered the rodeo. They wore flowered leis on their hats. They looked different from the other cowboys. People were not sure what to expect from these men from Hawai'i.

The rodeo lasted two days, and thousands of people watched the event. The three paniolo roped cattle with some of the best cowboys in the United States. In the end, Purdy came in first place. He roped a steer in 56 seconds. Ka'au'a and Low placed third and sixth. The men proved their skills to the mainland cowboys. They showed people that paniolo should be respected.

The three paniolo returned home to Hawai'i. They were met at the dock by fans. Everyone celebrated the three men. Parties and parades were held in their honor.

Eben Law, Archie Ka'au'a, Ikua Purdy, and Jack Low pose for a photo during the Cheyenne Frontier Days in 1908.

LET'S EXPLORE MATH

Barrel racing is a modern rodeo event in which people ride horses in patterns around barrels. The fastest time wins, but a 5-second penalty is added for each barrel that is knocked over. Write an expression for the score earned by each of these riders in a barrel-racing event.

1. Anne and her horse finished the course in 17 seconds and knocked over 2 barrels.

2. Jake and his horse finished the course in 19 seconds and knocked over 1 barrel.

3. Dennis's score in the event is represented by the expression $14 + (3 \times 5)$. Describe what Dennis and his horse did to earn this score.

Paniolo Culture

Over time, the original three cowboys returned to the mainland. Yet their skills, customs, and culture stayed in Hawai'i. When you look around Hawai'i, you can see paniolo culture. You see it in decorated saddles. You see it in the wide-brimmed hats that paniolo wear. Even the word *paniolo* has become part of the culture. It is a reminder of the cowboys who spoke Spanish.

Paniolo culture is in Hawaiian music, too. Mexican cowboys introduced guitars to the island. They brought guitars from the mainland. Paniolo worked hard. Playing guitar was a good way to relax after a long day.

Songs are also a way to tell stories. Paniolo sang about what they did in their lives. Some songs told stories about ranch life. One song might be about moving cattle up a hill. Another song might be about herding cattle into the sea. The songs were about the people, animals, and special events in the life of a cowboy.

People have written many songs about the island cowboys. One song is called *Waiomina* (WHY-oh-mee-nuh). This song tells the tale of the 1908 Wyoming rodeo. Another song, *Ku'u Hoa Hololio* (KOO-oo HOH-uh hoh-loh-LEE-oh), is about the friendship between a young paniolo and his horse.

Kalei Carralho, a paniolo, is a tour guide on the Kohala Mule Trail Adventure.

A paniolo herds cattle into a corral.

A guitarist plays in the slack-key style.

A musician plays the guitar during the Slack Key Guitar Festival.

Mexican cowboys brought the guitar to Hawai'i. However, Hawaiians created a special way of playing the guitar. It is called slack key. In this style, the six strings of the guitar are loosened. They aren't wound as tightly as normal guitars. Slack-key guitars have a very unique sound. They sound like two guitars playing at the same time.

Mexican cowboys also influenced the way Hawaiians sing. In Mexico, **falsetto** singing is popular. Falsetto is when someone sings in a very high-pitched voice. Cowboys brought this style of singing to the islands.

In Hawai'i today, this kind of singing is known as high voice. It sounds a lot like yodeling. Most Hawaiian falsetto singers are men. Some women sing this way, too.

Hawaiian culture has been shaped by various styles of music. The music of Hawai'i combines the songs of the paniolo with church songs and ancient Hawaiian chants. This mixture of influences creates a unique sound—a distinct blend featuring the slack key and steel guitar.

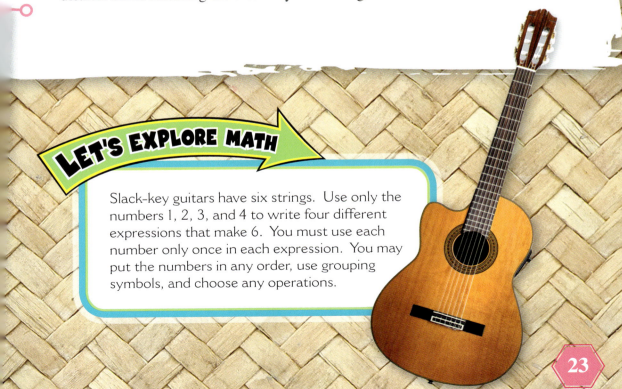

LET'S EXPLORE MATH

Slack-key guitars have six strings. Use only the numbers 1, 2, 3, and 4 to write four different expressions that make 6. You must use each number only once in each expression. You may put the numbers in any order, use grouping symbols, and choose any operations.

Paniolo Today

Paniolo still work on ranches on several Hawaiian islands. Ranching is a big industry. In Hawai'i, over one million acres of land are used for ranching. That is about one-fourth of the state's land mass! Hawai'i has two of the biggest ranches in the United States. Parker Ranch is one of the largest private cattle ranches. It is in Waimea (why-MAY-uh) on the Big Island. It has 130,000 acres of land with 26,000 cattle.

Many paniolo can trace their ranching roots back several **generations**. They come from a long line of paniolo. They do much of the same ranch work that their grandparents did. But, modern paniolo have tools that their **ancestors** did not. They have things like All-Terrain Vehicles (ATVs) and pickup trucks to help them. Paniolo no longer lead cattle into the water and onto ships. They stopped doing that in the 1940s. Instead, many ranches use large cargo planes to move cattle long distances.

A rider gets ready to demonstrate her rope skills at a rodeo on Moloka'i.

Dick Penhallow and Charlie Icamura proudly pose with a prize-winning bull from Parker Ranch.

Yutaka Kimura and his son Charlie were both head cowboys at Parker Ranch.

LET'S EXPLORE MATH

With 26,000 heads of cattle, Parker Ranch earns its reputation as one of the United States's largest ranching operations. Write the exponents to complete the powers of 10 that make each equation true.

1. $10^{\square} \times 26 = 26{,}000$
2. $10^{\square} \times 260 = 26{,}000$
3. $10^{\square} \times 2{,}600 = 26{,}000$

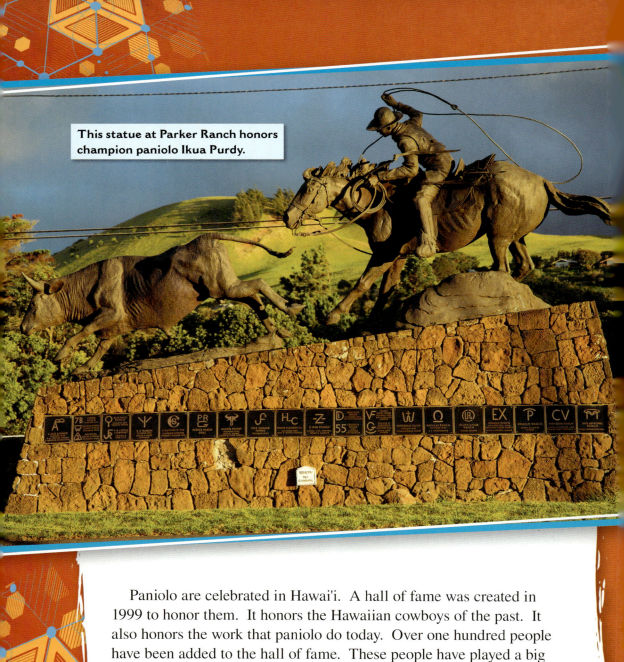

This statue at Parker Ranch honors champion paniolo Ikua Purdy.

Paniolo are celebrated in Hawai'i. A hall of fame was created in 1999 to honor them. It honors the Hawaiian cowboys of the past. It also honors the work that paniolo do today. Over one hundred people have been added to the hall of fame. These people have played a big part in paniolo culture and heritage.

Hawaiians also celebrate paniolo in other ways. Parades and events are held to honor cowboys every year. One of the biggest events takes place on Maui (MOW-ee) every Fourth of July weekend. The rodeo has been held for more than 50 years!

Hawai'i has good reason to celebrate paniolo. Cowboys have played a big role in the history and culture of the islands.

They have helped Hawaiians take care of the islands that they call home. Hawaiians have a rich history of being **stewards** of their islands. They are loyal protectors of the land. They are linked to the land in body and spirit.

The phrase *aloha 'aina* (uh-LOH-hah EYE-nuh) means "love of the land." It is a central idea in Hawaiian culture. Aloha 'aina is alive and well in Hawai'i. It is alive and well with paniolo.

Islanders from the Big Island of Hawai'i dress in flowers for parades celebrating their culture.

Problem Solving

The town of Makawao (MAH-kah-wow) on Maui has held parades and rodeos honoring paniolo traditions for more than 50 years. The parade features costumed riders on horseback, decorated floats, classic cars, marching bands, musical groups, and the rodeo queen and princesses. The parade always starts with keiki (KAY-kee), or children, "riding" stick horses.

Imagine that you are on the planning committee for a parade like the one in Makawao. Organize the parade by using the table to solve the problems.

1. Write and evaluate an expression showing the total number of people in cars and floats.

2. Write and evaluate an expression showing the total number of musicians.

3. Describe what the expression $(5 \times 15) + (2 \times 9) + 40$ shows.

4. How many total horses (not including stick horses!) will be in the parade? How do you know?

5. The planning committee is giving flowered leis to each person in the parade. Write and evaluate an expression to show how many leis are needed.

28

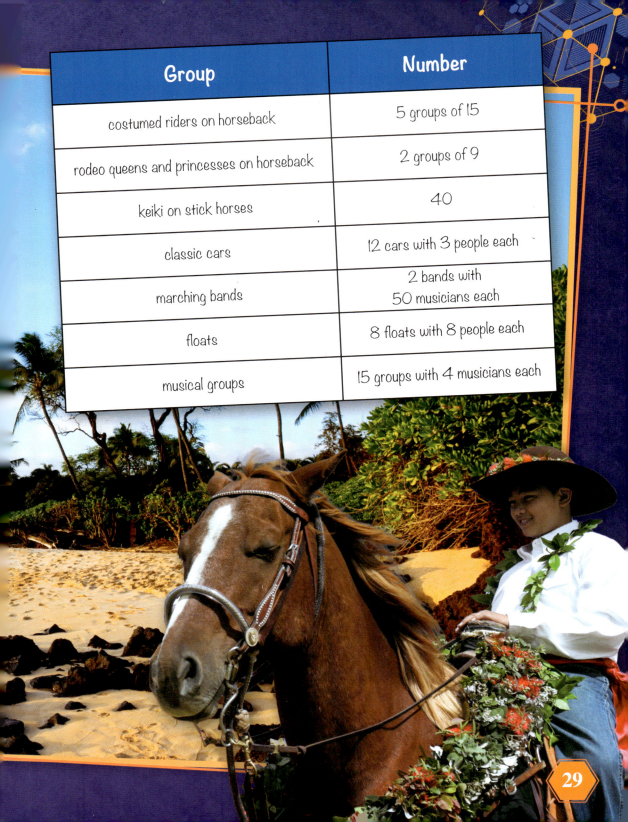

Group	Number
costumed riders on horseback	5 groups of 15
rodeo queens and princesses on horseback	2 groups of 9
keiki on stick horses	40
classic cars	12 cars with 3 people each
marching bands	2 bands with 50 musicians each
floats	8 floats with 8 people each
musical groups	15 groups with 4 musicians each

Glossary

ancestors—family members who lived before us

cattle—cows, bulls, or steers raised for food and kept on a ranch

chaps—leather leg coverings that are worn over pants

domesticate—to breed, train, and tame an animal

falsetto—a very high voice used by a man or woman while singing

generations—all of the people at the same stage who descended from a common ancestor

ideal—standard of excellence

indigenous—living naturally in a particular region or environment

lariats—long ropes used to catch livestock

leis—necklaces made of flowers

mainland—a large area of land that does not include islands

mammals—animals that feed milk to their young and have hair

ranching—raising cattle on a ranch

reproduce—to create babies

sombreros—wide-brimmed hats often worn in Mexico and the southwestern United States

stamina—ability to continue an activity for an extended period of time

stewards—people who protect things

taboo—not acceptable to talk about or do

tallow—fat from cattle used for making candles and soap

Index

aloha 'aina, 27
Big Island, 6, 9–10, 12, 16, 24, 27
Cleveland, Richard, 10
guitar, 20, 22–23
Ka'au'a, Archie, 18–19, 26
Kamehameha I, King, 6–7, 9–10
Kamehameha III, King, 10–11
kapu, 9–10
Kona, 9
Kossuth, 12
Louzeida, 12
Low, Jack, 18–19, 26
Maui, 27–28
Makawao, 28
music, 20, 23
O'ahu, 16
Pacific Ocean, 6
Parker Ranch, 13, 24–25
Purdy, Ikua, 18–19, 26
Ramon, 12

slack key, 22–23
Vancouver, George, 6–7, 9
Waimea, 24
Wyoming, 18, 20

Answer Key

Let's Explore Math

page 7:

The monk seals weigh 8 times what they did at birth because 8 × (25 + 27) is 8 times as great as 25 + 27, or there are 8 groups of 25 + 27.

page 13:
1. 13 × (4 − 2) = 26
2. (26 + 13) ÷ 3 = 13
3. (13 − 4) × 3 = 27
4. 27 ÷ (9 − 6) + 4 = 13

page 17:

A, D, E

page 19:
1. 17 + (2 × 5)
2. 19 + (1 × 5) or 19 + 5
3. Dennis and his horse finished the course in 14 seconds and knocked over 3 barrels, earning a 5 second penalty for each barrel.

page 23:

Expressions will vary. Examples include: 3 × 4 ÷ 2 × 1; (4 − 2) × 3 × 1; (4 + 3) − (2 − 1); 4 × 2 − (3 − 1)

page 25:
1. 10^3
2. 10^2
3. 10^1

Problem Solving
1. (12 × 3) + (8 × 8); 100
2. (2 × 50) + (15 × 4); 160
3. The expression is showing the total number of riders on horseback, including children on stick horses. There are 5 groups of 15 costumed riders, 2 groups of 9 rodeo queens and princesses, and 40 children on stick horses.
4. 93 horses; (5 × 15) + (2 × 9) = 93
5. (5 × 15) + (2 × 9) + 40 + (12 × 3) + (2 × 50) + (8 × 8) + (15 × 4); 393 leis are needed.